G000018049

THE LIFE & TIMES OF
MARTIN LUTHER KING

THE LIFE & TIMES OF

Martin Luther King

BY
A Noble

This edition printed for, Shooting Star Press Inc, 230
Fifth Avenue, Suite 1212, New York, NY 10001

Shooting Star Press books are available at special discount
for bulk purchases for sales promotions, premiums, fund-
raising or educational use. Special editions or book
excerpts can also be created to specification. For details
contact – Special Sales Director, Shooting Star Press Inc.,
230 Fifth Avenue, Suite 1212, New York, NY 10001

This edition first published by Parragon Books
Produced by Magpie Books Ltd, 7 Kensington Church
Court, London W8 4SP
Copyright © Parragon Book Service Ltd 1994
Cover picture & illustrations courtesy of: Rex Features;
Associated Press.

ISBN 1 57335 041 9
A copy of the British Library Cataloguing in Publication
Data is available from the British Library.

Typeset by Hewer Text Composition Services, Edinburgh
Printed in Singapore by Printlink International Co.

Martin Luther King was one of those extra-ordinary historical figures who make their mark on the world's consciousness without ever holding any senior political or military position. With Malcolm X, he brought race relations to the fore, shaming the conscience of white America, and ultimately that of white people generally. The effect he had was felt world-wide – such institutions as the Commission for Racial Equality in the UK owe their existence in part to his stand. His work is by no means complete, either in the United States or Europe, but without him racial integration, or at least harmony, would have made even less progress.

At the time of his birth, much ground had been lost by the black population in the United States. Shortly after the American Civil War (1861–65), blacks in the South had received the vote together with their liberty. This however had been withdrawn from them gradually by the Southern states, and their freedom turned out to be an illusion as they became sharecroppers, allowed to farm a small area of their employer's land in return for working on the rest of it – which was no better than slavery, and in some ways worse, as their employers no longer felt any need to look after them. Most were paid in kind rather than cash,

which severely restricted their independence. There was also the illegal 'peonage'
system, where poor blacks paid off debt by
work rather than cash, which kept them in
thrall to white Southern farmers.

Segregation laws, the 'Jim Crow' laws, were
introduced – black people could not eat at
the same counters as white people in restaurants or travel in the same part of the bus, for
example – and whites and blacks were
forbidden to marry each other (people were
defined as 'black' in some states if they had
any black ancestors). Education for blacks
was kept to a minimum to ensure that they
remained unskilled cheap labour to work the
cotton, tobacco and rice fields. Lynching was
commonplace, as an effective means of
terrorizing the black population, keeping it
cowed and submissive.

UPBRINGING OF A LEADER

Martin Luther King jun. was born on 15 January 1929 into a respectable, comfortably off family. His father, Martin Luther King sen. ('Daddy' King) was the pastor at the Ebenezer Baptist Church. The church was the most important black institution at the time; it was the one place where blacks could feel truly free and equal, where they could express themselves without fear of restraint. Congregations at churches such as Ebenezer numbered in the thousands, as people sought an oasis from the hostile world outside.

The black church espoused the values of self-help. It believed that if blacks made efforts to educate themselves, to act responsibly and work hard, they would earn the respect of whites, and so achieve equality. Almost to the end of his life, King shared this belief. Ministers were part of the small black middle class which had developed in the black community and ghettos: slowly the black community had developed its own commerce, run by black business men and entrepreneurs, and its own education system, including higher education. These developments, though, were separate from white institutions.

Daddy King was a strict father, but nonetheless King remembered his childhood as a happy time, living in a close-knit family. His first encounter with racism was at the age of six, when he was told by the father of a white friend that they could no longer play together because King was 'coloured'. This came as a shock to King; after he had run home, his parents explained to him the history of slavery and the cruelty of whites to blacks. They also made an important point: 'Don't let it make you feel you are not as good as white people. You are as good as anyone else and don't you forget it.' The instilling of self-respect among black people was one of King's (and Malcolm X's) dominant themes. Until blacks truly *felt* equal they could not *be* equal. His father set a strong example, refusing to truckle to whites. When stopped by a white policeman who said, 'Boy, show me your licence,' Daddy King pointed at his son and said, 'That's a boy there. I'm a man. I'm Reverend King.'

King's immediate reaction to this incident, and the harrowing history he heard immediately afterwards, was to hate all whites. But hating anybody went against Christian teaching – 'love thine enemy' and 'love thy neighbour' – as his parents frequently reminded him, and led to much internal tension in King during his adolescence. Martin Luther King sen. also took his duties as a minister beyond simply serving his church, believing that there should be no divide between religion and politics. As well as developing his business interests, he was also involved in voter registration drives and with the National Association for the Advancement of Colored People (NAACP), and this broader approach was to be adopted by his son.

The young King was a voracious reader: he had a fascination with words from an early age, and this was to stand him in good stead as an orator. His progress through school was extremely fast – he jumped two grades (in the US system, schoolchildren go through a grade a year) and went to Morehouse College, a theological college, at the age of fifteen. It was at Morehouse that he shed his blanket dislike of whites, as he worked there in some interracial groups. He also worked with white farm labourers during the vacation and began to realize that many of the blacks' problems were due to the fact that they were poor as well as due to racism. Morehouse is in Connecticut in the northern USA, where there were no segregation laws or open racism (as he was to find out later, racism in the North was much subtler than in the South). Going back to the South was an unpleasant experience.

At Morehouse, King had some doubts as to the value of religion, especially where it seemed to conflict with modern ways of thinking. He also found the style of fundamentalist black religion over-emotional: 'I had doubts that religion was intellectually respectable. I revolted against the emotionalism of Negro religion, the shouting and the stamping.' But the President of Morehouse, Benjamin Mays, and the Professor of Religion, George Kelsey, were able to convince King of the relevance of religion to the civil-rights struggle. Consequently, at the age of eighteen, he forsook ideas of becoming a lawyer or doctor, in favour of becoming a minister. At nineteen he was ordained.

With a degree in sociology under his belt, King then went to Crozer Theological Seminary, in Chester, Pennsylvania, to study for a degree in divinity. Here King encountered the ideas of such radical Christian thinkers as Walter Rauschenbusch and Reinhold Niebuhr. Rauschenbusch argued that the church should seek to establish Christian socialism, to overturn the evils of the capitalist state. Niebuhr, writing just after the horrors of the First World War, said that existing political structures reinforced man's immorality, and that they could only be overthrown by force, whether they manifested as class oppression within society or imperialism. King also learnt about Gandhi's non-violent protests against the British raj in

India. At Crozer, King performed brilliantly, coming top of his class: he was determined to prove that he was as good as the next man. He was a popular student, showing a tolerant attitude to incidents of racism, and was elected president of the student body. He graduated in 1951, leaving to study for a doctorate in systematic theology at Boston University.

At Boston he was exposed to the teachings of 'evangelical liberalism', which rejected fundamentalism, putting forward instead ideas of how Christianity could be an effective force for good in modern society. He also read Edgar S. Brightman's philosophy of personalism, that God was a personal, not an abstract spirit, and that within all people there was a capacity for good, which could be brought out by religious faith. Bound in

The Reverend Martin Luther King

Martin Luther King and his wife Coretta

with this philosophy were ideas of worth and self-respect that the black church has always tried to foster and with which King was familiar.

When he completed his doctoral studies, many positions were open to him, either as a teacher at Crozer or as a pastor in the North. But King felt that he owed it to his southern compatriots to return home, at least for a few years, to put something back into the community in which he had grown up. His new wife, Coretta, had wanted to stay in the North to pursue a singing career, but King overrode her wishes.

King sen. wanted King jun. to work with him at Ebenezer Baptist Church, but King jun. rejected this – he wanted to establish himself independently, and chose instead to work at Dexter Avenue Baptist Church in Montgomery, Alabama.

It was in Montgomery that King was to have leadership thrust upon him.

THE MONTGOMERY BUS BOYCOTT

Throughout most of his life, King was not really a radical political activist. He had been brought up in an essentially conservative environment, largely protected from the worst of racism. His family had middle-class values, virtually indistinguishable from those of their white counterparts, and his education, while it exposed him to new ideas, was conventional. King was too young to have been part of the Southern Negro Youth

Congress, a politically active group, and by the time he was at college, the Cold War had begun and McCarthyism – the ruthless exposure and persecution of anybody with Communist sympathies – had forced ideological left-wingers to lie low. The FBI under Edgar Hoover relentlessly harassed anybody it suspected, and the net of suspicion, with the prevailing paranoia about the Red Menace of Communist Russia, was cast wide. Even social democracy was regarded as a threat.

Dexter Avenue Baptist Church was exactly where one would have expected someone with King's education and upbringing to be the minister. It was attended mainly by the educated black middle class, most of whom were graduates, many working at Alabama State College. King was able to use his academic experience to be an intellectual rather than an emotional pastor – he was not one who 'whooped and hollered'. Once installed, he set about organizing his congregation: there was a cultural committee 'to lift the general cultural appreciation of our church and community', a scholarship committee to help bright students to attend college, and a Social and Political Action Committee, of which he said: 'Since the gospel of Jesus is a social gospel as well as a personal gospel . . . a Social and Political Action Committee shall be established [to keep] the congregation intelligently informed concerning the social, political and economic situation.' He thought the church should take an active role in community life, helping it to improve itself. As a minister with a divine vocation, he intended to control its activities: 'leadership never ascends from the pew to the pulpit, but it invariably descends from the pulpit to the pew.' King's interest in the community and his effective oratory – he spent fifteen hours a week preparing his sermons – made him a popular and respected figure, which was very gratifying to his father.

Montgomery was in the Southern heartland – it was there that Jefferson Davis had been made President of the Confederacy. Its segregation laws were particularly strict – there were even two separate taxi systems, and on the buses, which had white drivers, the blacks had to sit at the back, often paying at the front and entering at the rear. Drivers were renowned for their rudeness to blacks, and had even been known to shoot black passengers if they protested in any way. If more whites boarded than there was room for in the white section, blacks had to give up their seats, whereas if there were no whites on board, blacks were not allowed to sit on the empty seats. Blacks and whites could not sit in the same row, so if one seat was taken up by a white all of the blacks in the row had to move and stand. Justifiably, resentment at these rules ran pretty high, and where possible, blacks avoided travelling on the buses. Nonetheless, 70 per cent of passengers were black.

A boycott was first mentioned in Montgomery after Claudette Colvin, a fifteen-year-old schoolgirl, was dragged off a bus, handcuffed and put in jail for refusing to give up her seat to a white passenger. There had been a boycott in Baton Rouge, Louisiana, in 1953, but this had ended after a week. On 1 December 1955, Rosa Parks refused to give up her seat to a white, was taken to jail, and the Montgomery Bus Boycott was under way.

On 5 December the local black ministers met to discuss organizing a boycott. King, although only twenty-six, was elected their spokesman. There were probably two main reasons for this: first, none of the other black ministers wished to expose themselves and, second, because King as a recent arrival in Montgomery was not identified with any of the factions there. Out of this meeting came the Montgomery Improvement Association. King was given twenty minutes to prepare his address, to be given to about 5,000 at Holt Street Baptist Church. There were two major thrusts to his speech: democracy and the overthrow of oppression. 'We are here in a general sense because, first and foremost,

A black pupil is barred from entering
a whites-only school

The Reverend King tells of the struggle to come

we are American citizens, and we are determined to acquire our citizenship to the fullness of its meaning. We are here also because of our deep-seated belief that democracy transformed from thin paper to thick action is the greatest form of government on earth.' He wanted blacks to stand up for themselves: 'And, you know, my friends, there comes a time when people get tired of being trampled over by the iron feet of oppression . . . [they] get tired of being flung across the abyss of humiliation . . . [they] get tired of being pushed out of the glittering sunlight of life's July, and left standing amidst the piercing chill of an Alpine November. We are here this evening because we are tired now.' King also appealed to their self-discipline. They had to pursue their demands without violence. He knew that violent protest would stand no chance – blacks were only 10 per cent of the US population, and the apparatus of government, with its brutal state-troopers and National Guard, was well equipped to suppress physical protest. The Christian tradition with which his audience was imbued meant that this appeal was complied with.

The boycotters made three demands of the bus company: first come first served, with blacks filling up buses from the rear, black bus-drivers and better manners from white drivers. These requests were hardly revolutionary, yet the bus company and the city refused to agree to them. Integration had not been asked for, just fairer segregation. King knew that it would be too dangerous to call for full integration at this stage in the South.

The MIA organized a car pool, which the

police began to harass, arresting black drivers, including King. Dynamite was thrown at King's house. A black crowd confronted the mayor and the Commissioner of Public Safety and the police. King arrived in the nick of time to defuse the tension, and remove the possibility of violence. On 1 February the MIA's lawyer challenged the Alabama segregation laws in a federal court. At the end of February a local grand jury charged the MIA's leadership – over a hundred people – with breaking a 1921 anti-boycott law. Rather than wait to be arrested, the leaders, eighty-nine of them, presented themselves at the court-house in front of a cheering crowd. Twenty-four of them were ministers, who had overcome their earlier reluctance, when shown the support of their congregation. The church had turned out to be the ideal hub of the

MIA as ministers were not tied to any intimidating employers, and the churches were in contact with virtually the entire black community.

The boycott began to attract national and international interest, with journalists frequently visiting King. The NAACP became involved, as did the Fellowship of Reconciliation, the former seeking to broaden the demands of the protest, and the latter helping explain Gandhi's philosophy of non-violence to the Montgomery movement. King began to see the protest as part of a larger movement – the rising up of the oppressed world-wide – and as a part of a larger struggle for justice rather than for Montgomery alone:

'Integration is the great issue of our age . . . We are in the midst of a great struggle, the consequences of which will be world-shaking. But our victory will not be a victory for Montgomery's Negroes alone. It will be a victory for justice, a victory for fair play and a victory for democracy.'

The boycott continued for 381 days. The Supreme Court banned segregation and served an order to this effect on Montgomery's white officials on 20 December 1956. King received world-wide acclaim. Though he had not put himself forward as a leader, he had been more than a spokesman; by establishing the principle of non-violence he had given the boycott a moral dimension, which elevated it, and him, above the level of mere protest. He received many awards, including one from the NAACP, and provided the cover story for *Time* magazine on 18 February 1957,

which symbolized the approval of Northern
white liberal America.

Shortly after the end of the boycott, King,
with some encouragement from his advisers,
was instrumental in the founding of the
Southern Christian Leadership Conference
(SCLC), whose aim was to banish segregation. It was to be a non-violent movement,
as King had the utopian idea of a 'beloved
community' in which blacks and whites
lived in harmony. The SCLC was founded
with practical assistance and financial aid
from the Northern liberal community. The
SCLC was also formed to inherit the mo-
mentum of the Montgomery community
protest. The NAACP, while still effective,
confined most of its efforts to legal demoli-
tion of unfair race-laws. This approach had
many drawbacks. While having the laws

Peaceful demonstrators are stoned by angry whites

At the White House after the March on Washington

changed was of value, it did not have the moral effect of mass protest, and many Southerners were able to avoid the spirit of legal change, making some of the laws unenforceable (for example, in some states blacks were still segregated on buses for several years after the success in Montgomery because they did not have the nerve, as yet, to challenge local custom). Also, a resort to a legal attack on racism was extremely expensive, because the state system meant that each point had to be proved in each city; furthermore, some Southern states resorted to legally banning the NAACP itself, putting an almost insuperable legal obstacle in its way and causing a catastrophic decline in membership in the Southern states. State officials even demanded lists of NAACP members so that they could harass them more effectively.

The black church was to some extent protected from this, as it commanded respect even from Southern whites, and as it was not a corporation – which the NAACP was – it was free of government regulation. Despite being an integrationist organization, the SCLC was staffed entirely by blacks; this was partly to prevent infiltration by Communist whites (which would have brought the whole movement to an early end) and partly a matter of pride. The bus boycott had shown the blacks that they could work successfully together against an oppressive majority; they had earned their self-respect and running their own organization was a means of maintaining it. Finally the existence of the SCLC gave the lie to the Southern white contention that Southern blacks were basically content and only protested due to the interference of Communist agitators.

SPREADING THE WORD

King was now the unchallenged leader of the integrationist movement, seen as such by most outsiders. It had been hoped that the Montgomery boycott would spread to other cities, but this did not happen, as blacks pursued their rights through the courts rather than through protest. The Montgomery boycott had been a great success, but it had placed great demands on the community, both in terms of self-restraint and unity. Once the crisis was over, the movement dissolved into internal conflict. The NAACP also disliked having its position as the blacks' representative organization usurped and put many obstacles in the SCLC's way, placing hostile stories in the press and in general belittling its effectiveness. King hoped to recruit the Baptist Church throughout the South, in particular by ensuring the election of a friend, Gardner C. Taylor, to the presidency of the National Baptist Convention, the church's umbrella-organization. But he failed in this, and the conservative incumbent, Joseph H. Jackson, kept his position. So King had to fall back on recruiting individual black ministers to his cause, and in this he had some success. Many, though, were passive in the civil-rights struggle, not wishing to do anything that might jeopardize their comfortable lives, and this made King increasingly angry. He also had to divide his efforts between trying to develop a mass movement in the South, and raising money from liberals in the North.

In 1957, the SCLC diverted its attention to voter registration. King believed that change could be effected through democratic methods, and that it was essential that blacks took advantage of the right to vote. The 1957 Civil Rights Act redressed the fact that they did not have the vote in many states. But the response to the registration drive was disappointing. He was also disappointed by the lethargy of both parties, the Democrats and Republicans, in Congress. They had capitulated to the prejudices and undemocratic practices of the Southern 'dixiecrats' and 'to the blatant hypocrisy of right-wing, reactionary northerners'. It seemed to him extraordinary there was so little will to enforce the Constitution – as it said in the Declaration of Independence, the founding document of the United States: 'All men are created equal'. Not white men or black men or brown men, but all men. King warned both parties that he was here to stay:

'We come humbly to say to the men in the forefront of our government that the civil-rights issue is not an ephemeral, evanescent domestic issue that can be kicked about by reactionary guardians of the status quo. It is rather an eternal, moral issue which may well determine the destiny of our nation . . . The clock of destiny is ticking out. We must act now before it is too late.'

He could not tolerate the failure of the white population to see the clear moral position – people should only be judged by character, not the colour of their skin – which was clearly stated in their own avowed democratic principles. Given their moral failure, they could not act to redress the situation too soon: 'We call for a liberalism from the North which will be thoroughly committed to the ideal of racial justice and will not be deterred by the propaganda and subtle words of those who say, "Slow up for a while, you are pushing too fast."' His appeal to the conscience of white America was unrelenting: 'America must rid herself of segregation not alone because it is politically expedient, but because it is morally right!' When whites objected that one could not legislate behaviour, as in fact had been shown by the subtle ways in which Southern states maintained *de facto* segregation, he had a ready answer: 'You can't legislate integration but you can certainly legislate desegregation.' He realized that a change in white attitudes could only come through education. He also observed that legislation could stop the lynching of blacks – 'And I think that's pretty important also!'

King's world-wide reputation was growing, despite the slow progress the SCLC was making. He received many honours and awards and met many leading figures – Nkrumah in Ghana, Nehru in India – President Eisenhower and Vice-President Nixon – and Nelson Rockefeller and Averell Harriman, the challengers for the governorship of New York. He appealed to the Ghanaians and the Indians because they were emerging from their own freedom struggles, and he appealed to these conservative American whites because he led a non-political protest movement whose language was one they identified with – that of the American Constitution and the American dream. It was fully his intention to keep the race issue to the fore and not to cloud his message by associating himself with other radical political movements. Nor, given the Cold War atmosphere, did King wish to give his enemies any chance to accuse his movement of Communist influence.

In 1960 King became involved in the 'sit-in' movement, whereby black students would go to cafés or department-store restaurants and demand service. This form of protest had been initiated in Greensboro, North Carolina, in February, with more and more black college-students joining in. Around 70,000 people were eventually involved and 4,000 were arrested. King was eventually persuaded to participate in Atlanta and he and fifty-one others were arrested and sent to jail in October. King then had to appear before an ultra-bigoted white judge who had earlier given him a one-year suspended sentence for driving in Georgia with Alabama licence plates (an extraordinary 'crime' in a free country). On the grounds that he had broken his probation, he was sentenced to four months' hard labour at Reidsville state prison. This was a terrifying prospect for King: clearly he was being victimized and he could not know how far the Southern authorities were prepared to go in eliminating him. Two days later, though, he was granted bail after the intervention of Senator Robert Kennedy, the future Attorney-General, and brother of the Presidential candidate. John Kennedy used this intervention to boost his campaign, and received Daddy King's support. Given that the election was

Black students enter a desegregated university for the first time

President Johnson signs the Civil Rights Bill

only won by 112, 000 votes – a minute majority in a country of over 200 million – the late swing of black voters might have earned some recompense from John Kennedy when he was elected. But the white South had also voted Democrat in surprisingly large numbers, and Kennedy thought their support more important, especially as some Southern senators chaired important committees. Thus the President's support was at best lukewarm, and his chosen route to civil-rights reform was through the courts, which was fairly ineffective. In some areas, like the desegregation of schools, progress was actually backwards, with fewer black children attending recently integrated white schools.

Black students again took the initiative, forming the Student Non-violent Coordinating Committee (SNCC) to try and speed up federal adoption of civil rights. They protested in some of the most reactionary and right-wing parts of the South. The students were beaten up, arrested, sent to jail, and shot, but they did not give up. The Congress of Racial Equality (CORE) started Freedom Rides, travelling with whites in mixed groups and trying to use all the facilities *en route*. Mobs attacked them, and at one point King was trapped inside a church by a white mob and US marshals had to intervene to prevent violence. The Alabama National Guard was taken into federal control to maintain order. When the 'Freedom Riders' reached Jackson, Mississippi, most of them were arrested for breach of the peace and jailed when they refused bail. This inspired many more 'Freedom Riders' to head for Jackson and overfill

the jails. The government wanted the protests to slow down, but King pointed out
that his people wanted freedom now. As a
result of the Freedom Rides, the Interstate
Commerce Commission outlawed segregation in 1961. But King was not involved
with the Freedom Rides as he was devoting
his time to developing his version of the
American dream, the 'beloved country'
where all citizens would live in harmony.

VICTORY IN BIRMINGHAM

The next major confrontation took place in the town of Albany, Georgia. King had not intended to take part in a protest but at the Shiloh Baptist Church there, he was carried away by the enthusiasm of the moment and agreed to march. But the Chief of Police in Albany, Laurie Pritchett, had made plans to deflate the protest. To avoid overcrowding the city jails, he had made arrangements for cells to be held open elsewhere, and had strictly instructed his men to avoid any

Martin Luther King receives the Nobel Peace Prize

In Montgomery after the five-day march from Selma

semblance of brutality. King managed to get himself arrested, but Pritchett, in a cunning move, released him, claiming that another black man had put up his bail money. Thereafter, the Albany movement petered out, without gaining any of its demands, and riven by internal dissension. Pritchett had prepared himself for King's tactics by reading his book *Stride Towards Freedom*, and was intelligent enough to realize that brutal handling of the demonstrations would lead to federal intervention, which was the gravest threat to Southern segregationists. Anticipating King's arrival, he had meticulously drilled his men for months so that they would handle the demonstrators effectively without violence.

The next flashpoint was Birmingham, Alabama. To avoid the mistakes of Albany, the

SCLC inner council met in Dorchester, Georgia, to plan the Birmingham campaign. They decided to attack segregation in department stores, thereby limiting the protest to what was attainable, rather than confronting the city government which would always put the views of the white electorate first. The Public Safety Commissioner in Birmingham was Eugene 'Bull' Connor, a dyed in the wool bigot and racist. Birmingham was renowned for its racism and was a fertile recruiting ground for the Ku-Klux-Klan. Bombing of black churches, murder and assault were condoned. The SCLC hoped to provoke Connor into violence to discredit him. Initially he showed unexpected restraint, though King was jailed. While in solitary confinement he read an attack on the aims of the protest by white clergymen, and in response wrote the 'Letter from Birmingham City Jail', which explained in great detail his methods and aims. It also set out the probable outcome of events if the non-violent protests were not heeded – King was not trying to blackmail whites with fear of a racial war, he was simply setting out what he foresaw as the result of continued oppression, and after all, Malcolm X and other firebrands constantly proposed more direct action (the American black Muslim movement believed very much in 'an eye for an eye'). The 'Letter' did much to persuade the Northern churches – over a million copies were printed – to follow their consciences and to urge demonstrations against racism, although the white Southern church was largely unmoved.

King was then tried by a local court, but as

the judge did not want him to become a
martyr he changed the charge from civil
contempt, whereby a defendant stayed in
jail until he apologized, to criminal contempt, which carried only a short sentence
and which was subject to a time-consuming
appeals procedure, during which a defendant
would remain free. King came out of jail to
find that the protest was not receiving the
wide support he had hoped for. James Bevel,
one of the new generation of young activists
in his team, suggested that they recruit
children to the campaign (some had in fact
already gone to jail). This was done and
thousands of black schoolchildren con-
verged on the starting-point for the demonstration. At this point Connor cracked, and
King achieved the sort of publicity that the
campaign craved.

Connor ordered his men to wade in brutally, setting dogs on demonstrators and bystanders alike, and having the fire service hose them down. Hundreds of children were arrested. This outrageous behaviour was fully reported in the world's media, and widely seen on TV in the US and overseas. (Television was relatively new at the time and the impact it made then was much stronger than it is now when disasters and riots across the world are almost daily fare.) The image it presented to the world of America's internal oppression was something that no country paying lip-service to democracy could tolerate. President Kennedy went on nation-wide television on 11 June. He declared civil rights to be a moral issue: '. . . as old as the Scriptures and as clear as the American Constitution. The heart of the question is whether all Americans are to be afforded equal rights and equal opportunities; whether we are going to treat our fellow Americans as we want to be treated.' He concluded by saying that he would take the issue to Congress and ask it 'to make a commitment it has not fully made this century to the proposition that race has no place in American life or law'. On 19 June a new Civil Rights Bill was submitted to Congress.

King was delighted. At last he seemed to have got the sort of commitment he wanted from the white Government. To keep the pressure up, and to ensure that the bill was passed 'without compromise or filibuster', it was decided that there would be a March on Washington for Freedom. To ensure the support of the NAACP, this was to be a non-violent protest. King, Wilkins of the NAACP, and other black leaders met with

The first interracial marriage in the Deep South

The motel in Memphis where King was shot

Kennedy to assure him that the demonstration would be fully controlled. Any hint of a repetition of the scenes of Birmingham in the nation's capital would have led to the event being banned. The leaders told the President that 100, 000 demonstrators were expected. In the event, 250, 000 turned up on 28 August 1963. By the Lincoln Memorial, King reminded his audience of Lincoln's Emancipation Proclamation – 'a great beacon-light of hope' – before continuing: 'But one hundred years later, the Negro is still not free . . . sadly crippled by the manacles of segregation . . . on a lonely island of poverty in the midst of a vast ocean of material prosperity.' Soon after, there was a cry from the audience: 'Tell us about your dream, Martin.' His prepared speech over, he fell back on the traditional rhetoric of the black Baptist preacher:

'I have a dream that one day this nation will rise up and live out the true meaning of its creed, "We hold these truths to be self-evident, that all men are created equal." . . . I have a dream that one day on the red hills of Georgia, sons of former slaves and sons of former slaveholders will be able to sit down together at the table of brotherhood. I have a dream that one day even the state of Mississippi, a state sweltering with the heat of injustice, sweltering with the heat of oppression, will be transformed into an oasis of freedom and justice . . . I have a dream that one day . . . in Alabama, little black boys and black girls will be able to join hands with little white boys and white girls as sisters and brothers . . .'

The crowd responded ecstatically to the sense and rhythm of his words. He finished with an appeal for freedom for all: 'Let freedom ring from the prodigious hilltops of New Hampshire . . . from the mighty mountains of New York . . . Let freedom ring from Stone Mountain of Georgia . . . from Lookout Mountain of Tennessee. Let freedom ring from every hill and molehill of Mississippi . . . And when this happens, and when we allow freedom to ring, when we let it ring from every village and every hamlet, from every state and every city, we will be able to speed up that day when all of God's children, black men and white men, Jews and Gentiles, Protestants and Catholics, will be able to join hands and sing in the words of the old Negro spiritual: "Free at last. Free at last. Thank God Almighty, we are free at last."'

But reaction was not slow in coming. Southern whites did not willingly surrender a system that favoured them so greatly. What particularly worried the black leaders too was the lack of support from Northern whites. George Wallace, the racist white candidate for presidential nomination from Alabama, won a third of the vote in Indiana and Wisconsin. Barry Goldwater received the Republican nomination; he had been one of only six senators to vote against the Civil Rights Bill, regarding it as socialist subversion. Racists in Birmingham bombed the Sixteenth Baptist Church and four girls were killed. The Ku-Klux-Klan organized its White Knights section which murdered three civil-rights workers, two of whom were white, on 21 June. Several other murders were perpetrated; when caught, the murderers were let off by white Southern juries.

Black leaders demanded that Washington do something to control the courts and ensure justice, but the Department of Justice claimed that it had no jurisdiction over local courts, and if juries acquitted defendants, then according to the law they were innocent. Meanwhile the FBI stood on the sidelines, watching as civil-rights leaders were physically attacked and marched off to jail. King accused the FBI of supporting Southern segregationists. This made him a marked man so far as J. Edgar Hoover, the FBI's Director, was concerned. Hoover embarked on a smear campaign. Obsessed with the threat of Communism, and using this threat to bolster his own position, he insisted that his agents find links between King and Communism. They duly did so. One agent wrote: 'We are in complete agreement with the Director that Communist influence is being exerted on Martin Luther King.' Using the police apparatus of the modern state, they spied in every way possible on his activities, seeking to discredit him in the eyes of his supporters. The FBI received permission to tap King's telephone and planted bugs wherever they thought he might be. They tried to paint a picture of an immoral King, engaging in numerous adulterous relationships. This failed when they wanted to plant stories in the papers; newspapers had a gentlemen's agreement not to expose the sexual peccadilloes of leading figures. Power had always been attractive to the opposite sex, and we now know, for example, that President Kennedy had numerous liaisons. At the time, in a more sexist world, these were regarded tolerantly, almost as one of the benefits of the job. So the FBI failed in this campaign.

James Earl Ray, King's assassin

Martin Luther King's funeral at his father's church

For the whole of 1963 and 1964 the FBI pursued King, and tried to prevent him receiving the honours and awards that increasingly were being showered on him. In January 1963 he was *Time* magazine's 'Man of the Year', the first black to receive the honour. President Johnson gave him an audience. In October 1964 he received the Nobel Prize for Peace. The city of Atlanta, despite the initial objections of whites, gave a dinner honouring King as Georgia's first Nobel Prize winner. Hoover was so infuriated by all of this that he attacked King on the record as 'the most notorious liar in America'. A few days later the FBI sent King a tape with a menacing message, effectively inviting him to commit suicide.

Hoover's persecution was very frightening to the protest movement, given the awe-

some power of the FBI, and that President
Johnson, who must have known of its
actions, did nothing. But Johnson probably did not in any way support the
campaign of vilification: the Hoover files
notoriously included damning information
on presidents as well as other suspects.
Johnson continued to give access to
King, thereby indicating his continuing
support. The FBI campaign made life
difficult for the SCLC and the freedom
movement as when negotiating they never
knew if the other side was privy to their
tactics, and of course it was sometimes
difficult to know if dissent was due to
agents provocateurs or not. Eventually,
though, King and his colleagues came to
joke about it, preaching directly to Hoover
when they found hidden microphones in
churches and asking agents to get off the

line when there was a poor telephone connection. Also, knowing that their activities were not secret, they reasoned that they had nothing real to fear from the FBI.

A BROADER STRUGGLE

The 1964 Civil Rights Act did not enfranchise all Southern blacks and King determined to make this his next aim. President Johnson wanted to slow down the pace of reform but King rejected this. The town he turned his attention to was Selma, where the voters were almost entirely white, despite the population being mostly black. The local sheriff, Jim Clark, was a typical bigoted redneck and responded in a predictable way to the demonstrations and marches,

A campaigner marks the first anniversary
of King's death

The struggle against racism continues

which had begun in early 1965, arresting large numbers of protesters. Protesters were also beaten and two were murdered.

On 7 March, 600 demonstators began a march from Selma to Montgomery. Clark's men, together with state troopers, mounted and on foot, brutally assaulted the marchers with batons, whips and tear-gas. All of this was seen on television and the reaction throughout America was sheer disgust at these repressive tactics. President Johnson called in federal troopers to protect the marchers, thereby for the first time showing Government support for the civil-rights campaign. Johnson had been thinking of a voting rights bill and the reaction of the nation spurred him on and the bill was presented to Congress on 6 August 1965. It seemed as if the civil-rights struggle was over. King, up to this stage, had firmly believed that society could be made fair through the power of the ballot-box. Undoubtedly achieving the vote was a major step in the right direction.

But King's perspective had always been that of the South. In the North, blacks had equal rights – no segregation, the vote – as whites, and yet their economic position was parlous. As Malcolm X pointed out, blacks were allowed to eat in restaurants with whites but didn't have the money to do so. They lived in filthy poverty-stricken ghettos, rife with crime, drug abuse, and general despair. More than half the black population of the United States lived in the North. Within days of the Voting Rights Bill being signed, on 11 August 1965, a massive outbreak of rioting occurred in the Watts ghetto of Los

Angeles. Forty-five square miles of the city were burnt to the ground, thirty-four people were killed and 4, 000 were arrested. 14, 000 National Guardsmen and 1, 600 policemen were drafted in to restore order.

Watts was a revelation to King. For the first time he realized that the economic problems of blacks were even more important than those of race discrimination. He began to see the ghetto as a 'system of internal colonialism', with blacks kept there in economic subjection by the ruling white class. He determined to take the non-violent protest movement to the North, starting in Chicago. But the response of urban blacks was minimal. Desperate to point out the *de facto* segregation existing in Chicago, King initiated marches through white areas of town. This alienated much of his white liberal support, and the residents in these districts showed their disapproval by pelting the marchers. Eventually Mayor Daley signed an agreement that discrimination by the housing and real-estate industry would cease, but did nothing to enforce this. King then embarked on a voter-registration campaign in the hope of using the black vote as a lever to pressure those in power. But in the 1967 mayoral election, Daley was re-elected for the fourth time, with the black vote being overwhelmingly in his favour.

The Vietnam War also began to absorb the Government's attention. King had refrained from speaking out against the war because this would have lost him Johnson's support, though he later regretted this. He felt that the war exposed capitalist America's repressive tendencies – after all, the war in Vietnam was a war of independence, just as America's had been nearly two hundred years earlier. The massive escalating cost of the war also meant an end to the War on Poverty initiative supposed to reduce the extreme economic inequality on the domestic front. King lost faith in the American dream: 'A nation that spends $500, 000 to kill one enemy soldier in Vietnam and only $50 to get one of its own citizens out of poverty is a nation that will be destroyed by its own moral contradictions.'

As a proponent of non-violence he found American methods in Vietnam especially abhorrent – defoliation, napalm, massive bombing of civilians. In New York, King denounced the war outside the UN building. Johnson was furious, as was most of the media. Riots broke out in Detroit and elsewhere, in which eighty-three people, mostly black, were killed. Whites were frightened by these eruptions of black anger, and took harsh countermeasures. Black Power was growing with its insistence on separate development from whites, and the abandonment of non-violence. Organizations like the SNCC and CORE adopted the Black Power cause, thereby losing white liberal financial support.

King decided that his real target should be economic injustice and began the Poor People's Campaign. Many of his advisers felt that the hint of socialism would provoke a backlash and were against the campaign. But on 18 March 1968 King went to Memphis in support of the dustmen who were striking for union recognition and a wage rise. He agreed to return on the 28th to lead a march to City Hall. The march, though, was badly organized and quickly degenerated into a riot. The police waded in and dispersed the marchers, one of whom was killed. King was devastated: it seemed to mean an end to his reputation as a non-violent leader. But his supporters persuaded him to carry on with the campaign, and to organize a more successful march. On 1 April they heard that Johnson would not be running for President again, and would start negotiations with North Vietnam. It began to look as if things might be going King's way again.

On 3 April he addressed a gathering of strikers in Memphis:

'Like anybody, I would like to live a long life . . . but I'm not concerned about that now. I just want to do God's will. And he's allowed me to go up to the mountaintop. And I've looked over. And I've seen the Promised Land. I may not get there with you, but I want you to know tonight that we as a people will get to the Promised Land. So I'm happy tonight. I'm not worried about anything. I'm not fearing any man.'

On 4 April, there was more good news – a federal judge had rejected the city's request that the march be banned. But it was too late; that evening, standing on his motel balcony talking with his colleagues, King was shot. We shall never know how successful his campaign against poverty might have been, and we may never know who conspired to assassinate him – it has been suggested that the FBI was involved, as it feared his becoming a black Messiah. His moral and inspirational stance made him a dominant figure in the struggle for human rights, one who had the respect of all blacks and most whites, even if they did not agree with him. In 1983, Congress recognized this by making his birthday a national holiday, just as are those of George Washington and Abraham Lincoln.

A good epitaph perhaps would be from one of his sermons at Ebenezer Church speaking against the Vietnam War, but applicable to his approach to any moral problem:

'I don't care who doesn't like what I say about it. I don't care who criticizes me in an editorial. I don't care what white person or Negro criticizes me. I'm going to stick with the best. On some positions, cowardice asks the question, "Is it safe?" Expediency asks the question, "Is it politic?" Vanity asks the question, "Is it popular?" But conscience asks the question, "Is it right?" And there comes a time when a true follower of Jesus Christ must take a stand that's neither safe nor politic nor popular, but he must take that stand because it is right.'

LIFE AND TIMES

Julius Caesar
Hitler
Monet
Van Gogh
Beethoven
Mozart
Mother Teresa
Florence Nightingale
Anne Frank
Napoleon

LIFE AND TIMES

JFK
Martin Luther King
Marco Polo
Christopher Columbus
Stalin
William Shakespeare
Oscar Wilde
Castro
Gandhi
Einstein

FURTHER MINI SERIES INCLUDE

ILLUSTRATED POETS

Robert Burns
Shakespeare
Oscar Wilde
Emily Dickinson
Christina Rossetti
Shakespeare's Love Sonnets

FURTHER MINI SERIES INCLUDE

HEROES OF THE WILD WEST

General Custer
Butch Cassidy and the Sundance Kid
Billy the Kid
Annie Oakley
Buffalo Bill
Geronimo
Wyatt Earp
Doc Holliday
Sitting Bull
Jesse James

FURTHER MINI SERIES
INCLUDE

THEY DIED TOO YOUNG

Elvis
James Dean
Buddy Holly
Jimi Hendrix
Sid Vicious
Marc Bolan
Ayrton Senna
Marilyn Monroe
Jim Morrison

THEY DIED TOO YOUNG

Malcolm X
Kurt Cobain
River Phoenix
John Lennon
Glenn Miller
Isadora Duncan
Rudolph Valentino
Freddie Mercury
Bob Marley